Frontispiece: **Sir Robert Grieve beside a portrait of Sir Patrick Geddes painted in the 1920s which is in his possession.**

GRIEVE ON GEDDES

**Professor Sir Robert Grieve's
Appreciation of the Effect of Sir Patrick
Geddes's Thinking on His Planning
Work in Scotland**

Published by
The Sir Patrick Geddes Memorial Trust

Distributed by
Mrs Anne Geddes
21 Swanston Place
Edinburgh
EH10 7DD

Designed and Produced
by
Scotland's Cultural Heritage
University of Edinburgh
Drummond Street
Edinburgh
EH1 1LZ

Photography: Jim Dallas

Cover Illustration: Willi Reid

Printed by
MD Print & Design
Unit 9 Castlebrae Business Centre
Peffer Place
Edinburgh

INTRODUCTION

This monograph has been written by one distinguished Scotsman about another; both have played a notable role in the development of town and regional planning; both are professors, and both have been knighted. There can scarcely be any topic of concern to Scots today in which these two wise countrymen of ours have not said or done or implied something relevant or thought provoking. It was therefore a good idea of the Sir Patrick Geddes Memorial Trustees to publish Sir Robert Grieve's assessment of the influence that Sir Patrick Geddes, a botanist and sociologist, had on him, a civil engineer and town planner.

Much has been written and is known about Patrick Geddes. He needs no introduction, but Helen Meller in her biography *Patrick Geddes*, published by Routledge, 1990, wrote that "the problem of assessing Geddes's impact on the nascent planning movement is not at all straightforward." Sir Robert certainly confirms this as he examines Geddes's influence on his own career.

Sir Robert, or Bob as he likes to be called, was born on 11 December 1910. His mother was half Highland, half Irish and his father, just like Geddes's, was a soldier. When he finished his engineering apprenticeship in 1933 he was unemployed for a year, qualifying as a Civil Engineer in 1935 and as a Town Planner in 1937.

Keeping himself fit in body and soul he took to the Hills and later became a skilled mountaineer and, eventually, president of the Scottish Mountaineering Club and of the Scottish Mountaineering Council. He also nourished his mind with the study of Scottish poetry which enlivens his speeches and conversation, charming all his listeners, and making him a star at planners' gatherings, here and abroad - he is the British founder member and Vice President of the International Society of City and Regional Planners.

Between 1943 and 1946 he became the lynch-pin of the Clyde Valley Plan which has been the most effective of all the post-war regional plans. He then went into the Scottish Office and was made Chief Planner in 1960. Geddes scorned officialdom and disdained political processes but Bob helped to persuade his

I

colleagues and their political masters that co-ordinated administration and the improvement of the environment were essential to pull Scotland out of its recurring recessions. He left the Civil Service in 1965 on being asked to take the newly created chair of Town and Regional Planning in the University of Glasgow. But later that year he was invited by the Secretary of State to be the first chairman of the Highlands and Islands Development Board - a politically sensitive role if ever there was one. In his own words he "exchanged the unexceptionable sentiment for the terror of action".

The Royal Town Planning Institute has only awarded its Gold Medal to eight people since 1914. Lewis Mumford, the American disciple of Geddes whose classic books self-confessedly put into words what Geddes thought about twentieth century problems was honoured in 1957 and Sir Robert Grieve in 1974. His retirement has been very productive. He was chairman of the BBC's Scottish Committee; of the Royal Fine Arts Commission for Scotland; of the Committee that produced the closely reasoned 'Claim of Right for Scotland' - the case for Devolution; and of the comprehensive Glasgow Housing Inquiry in 1988. This truly distinguished record was capped when in 1990 he received the Lord Provost of Glasgow's Award for Outstanding Public Service - a recognition from his own city which has given him more pleasure than any other award.

The trustees are very grateful to Bob for his labours and for the extreme care and thought he has put into this monograph. They are confident that it will rekindle an interest in Geddes's philosophy of planning. As Lewis Mumford wrote in the *Introduction to Patrick Geddes in India* (Lund Humphries, 1947), "The tasks that Geddes undertook as a solitary thinker and planner have become the collective task of our generation." It is Bob who has been leading us in this task. It is nothing less than the concerted action to enrich the lives of our fellow human beings through the improvement of their environment and the sustaining of their cultural roots.

F.P. TINDALL
F.D.N. SPAVEN

II

PROLOGUE

This monograph cannot, by its nature and length, be a biography of Geddes. A good number of biographies by very different authors have been published since the 1920s, the most comprehensive and detailed being those of Philip Boardman in 1978 and Helen Meller in 1990. Many general articles, essays, and specific theses about him and his work have been written, and are still being written. But it has been the understanding of the Geddes Memorial Trust, which asked me to produce this monograph, that I should write it because of my own past work on planning in Scotland; and that my Memorial Lecture in the Outlook Tower on the 50th anniversary of Geddes's death might be the basis of it. Indeed, so far as I know, nothing has yet been written by a Scottish planner who has worked all his life on a wide range of Scottish planning problems from the local to the national scale. So this essay is simply a vehicle carrying the story of the influence on me, eventually, of Geddes's teaching.

It is a very personal story; it is certainly not a heroic one. It is, rather, the abbreviated account of a real workaday planner manoeuvring within the inevitable constraints of a real legislative system; a planner who had to deal with the shifts and compromises of politics, central and local. In any Geddesian sense, he was inadequately trained and qualified. But he slowly became aware, directly and indirectly, of a stream of thought and action from an outstanding intellect outlining an approach to planning more perhaps in line with Heaven than the observable surrounding Earthiness of the aftermath of the British Industrial Revolution - Geddes's "Palaeotechnic Era".

Lord Holford's words at the Centenary of Geddes's birth in 1954 at the Outlook Tower - at which I was present - are appropriate enough to this essay: "I am here as President for the time being of the Town Planning Institute and for the simple reason that the Institute without Geddes would hardly have existed. As a trade union it might perhaps have come into existence; but as a voluntary association, a learned society, it would have had an insecure foundation without the work that Geddes did. Then I am

III

here as a teacher, to acknowledge him as the great educator and interpreter of the function of environmental planning in ordinary life . . . in the third place I am here just because I did *not* know Patrick Geddes in person, because I was never directly stimulated or exasperated by his prescriptions for regional survey, his proposals for conservative surgery, his plans for regional development. On the other hand I cannot escape his influence. The Greek epigram on Plato is applicable to him: 'Wherever I go in my mind I meet Geddes coming back!'"

I do not know when Holford first felt the impact of Geddes's teaching; for me, it was towards the end of the War of 1939-45. I realised through a series of flash-backs that my mind had already been illuminated indirectly by other general reading which I shall touch on later. These made mention, in memorable ways, of our environment, its history, its value, its beauty and utility and the contribution that man made to its nourishment and improvement. They underlined the inter-connection of all things and the need to attempt such a synthesis before any action by man took place within it. It was therefore not in a wholly unprepared state that one winter evening I was witness to a scene in Glasgow a few months before the death of Geddes on 17 April 1932. It remains in my mind as a vivid vignette.

On that evening I got off a bus at the top of Buchanan Street on my way to evening classes in the Royal Technical College (now Strathclyde University). Immediately north of where I stood lay an extensive area of the worst kind of slum, the Cowcaddens - now mercifully gone. And out of it, as I looked up the street before crossing, came a long procession of small stunted men with little cardboard banners . . . "We want work" . . . "We want bread." Silently, on the experimental rubber blocks of the street, they passed out of the darkness of the notorious Cowcaddens down into the bright lights of the central shopping area, not with the raised fists and rhythmic shouting of today - their physical stamina did not look up to that. And, silently, they were gone. I was 20 then. I knew nothing about Geddes; and was not going to hear anything about him at the "Tech" where I was bound. But I had seen a ghostly manifestation of what he called the Palaeotechnic Era.

GEDDES - THE MAN

Patrick Geddes was born at Ballater in the Eastern Highlands of Scotland on October 2nd, 1854; reared, educated and started work as a bank clerk in Perth; lived and had his base in the years of his manhood in Edinburgh; spent many years of his life working abroad, mainly in India during World War One; but died in Montpellier in France in 1932 beside the College des Ecossais which he conceived of, and set up, in 1924-25. His post-school education included a period at the Sorbonne in Paris, and under the famous Professor Huxley in London. Each period greatly affected his future work and beliefs on biology, evolution and the need for synthesis in thought and action in man's environment. He lived the last eight years of his life of 78 years at Montpellier.

His whole upbringing and education was Scottish. All through life his beliefs were coloured by the landscape, theology and psychology of the Scot, which emerged in many ways. In the period in which he and his wife Anna worked on the social and physical rehabilitation of the slums of the then High Street of Edinburgh (a process he called "conservative surgery" as distinct from wholesale demolition and rebuilding) his conversations and discussions with the inhabitants of those towering, ancient tenements were carried out in the local Scottish dialect. It was not the least part of his effect on them in his work of rehabilitation; Dostoevsky, in *The House of the Dead*, describing the ability to relate between social classes by using the local dialect, called this "a rare facility", a highly desirable kind of bilingualism, a bridge between classes.

Geddes's article in the First Quarterly Edition of the *Evergreen* (Spring 1895), of which he was Editor, clearly reflected his attitude to Scotland's place in the United Kingdom and the Scots' constantly recurring desire for some form of devolved government. It revolved around the extraordinary demonstration of Scottish patriotism which attended Professor John Stuart Blackie's funeral in 1875. In the article he said this: "Nor need we here speak of those who think that because we would not quarrel with Brother Bull, nor abandon our part in the larger responsibilities of united nationality and race, we must needs also sink the older loves and kinships, the smaller nationality, wholly." And this, ". . . but to this spoiling of what might be good Scots to make indifferent Englishmen natural selection will always continue to oppose some limit. Nor need we analyse the current forms of dull prosperity, of soul-deep hypocrisy so rife among us - in this 'east-windy west-endy town' above others - that routine-fixed intellect and frozen heart against which Blackie's very extravagances were part of his testimony"; and ". . . what then is this Scotland of ours? What life does it actually show? What ideas and what aims are nascent among its youth? What manner of history will they make; what literature will they write? And we - what counsel in thought, what initiative in action, can we offer them?"

These questions, written 100 years ago, are still valid and contemporary. They have not gone away and certainly will not go away.

Essentially, his whole way of life and opinion was based on the idea of the cosmopolitan Scot. He never forgot (and indeed relied on) his national and regional views in attempting to focus the international scene. The very word, international, is meaningless without nationalisms; and everything in world politics today heavily underlines that. His recipé for successful internationalism was paradoxically contained in Voltaire's phrase: "*Il faut cultiver votre jardin.*"

His very extensive journeys to various parts of the world, and his work in them, were a reflection of his constant propagation of the idea of regional survey and plan - to *know* what was fundamentally of the region, and to produce a strategy and administration which truly suited that region within the wider context. His regional analogies were always closely connected with the generalities of mankind. The whole life of the region had to be seen and studied against the triad of "Place, Work, Folk", which he had taken from the writings of the French sociologist, Le Play. It was largely on the foundation of this triad that he built up the elaborate diagrams—his "thinking machines", his "novum organon", which became central to his teaching of synthesis, of the inter-connectedness of all things and all thought. His authorship of works of substance was perhaps the lesser part of his effect on thinking. He wrote in a mannered and cumbersome style - a kind of sub-Carlylean English *(Cf. Quotations in* APPENDIX I), and he cannot be judged principally by his published works - except those of a purely scientific character. His effect on people was largely brought about by his talking, his lectures, and his unusual exhibitions and masques. Through these and his power of connected thinking and arresting phraseology he clearly left the lasting impression of a very remarkable personality.

It all fits in with the claim of his contemporaries that he was a charismatic human being who left an unforgettable impression wherever he went, whether in Jerusalem, Dublin, Cyprus or India. His own account of how he persuaded the Maharajah of Indore to appoint him as Maharajah for a day is perhaps the most telling - and amusing - example of this. He used his power that day to persuade and organise the people through a great Masque and procession to clean up the city as the first important step in the abolition of Cholera. And the procession was led by the "untouchables", the absolutely essential street-sweepers - a truly Geddesian touch!

As an endpiece to this chapter I think it best to make a lengthy quotation from his most famous disciple, the American who has written some of the best scholarly books on the growth and character of urban civilisation - Lewis Mumford. In an article written in 1928 (just four years before the death of Geddes) in *The Survey*, New York, entitled *Who is Patrick Geddes?* he had this to say about the Scottish polymath:

"If one dropped in on a luncheon group at the faculty club of a metropolitan university and asked a dozen scholars: Who *is* Patrick Geddes? there would probably be a dozen answers, and though some of the answers would be hazy, they would all, I think, be different; and one might get the impression that Professor Geddes is a vigorous institution, rather than a man. The biologist would probably be the first to speak up: he would say that Geddes, with his old pupil J. Arthur Thomson, the editor of the *Outline of Science*, had written the classic book on *The Evolution of Sex*, and in more recent years had collaborated on two fertile little volumes in the Home University Series. He might add . . . that Geddes had occupied the chair of Botany of St Andrews University for more than thirty years. The economist is a little more shaky in his knowledge; still, he might recall that Geddes had written on statistics and economic theory and co-operation in the eighties, and had only a year or two ago published a closely written pamphlet on *The Principle of Sociology in Relation to Economics*. At this point the sociologist might wake up: for him Geddes would be one of the main founders of the Sociological Society of Great Britain, the author of a series of papers published by that society on *Civics as Concrete and Applied Sociology*, the joint editor of a series of post-war books devoted to the *Making of the Future*; and if our sociologist were quite honest he would probably add that he had not read any of these essays . . . So it would go on. The geographer would think of Geddes as the founder of the regional survey movement, and the professor of city planning would put Geddes at the head of the Cities Movement in Great Britain, and indicate how Geddes' survey of Edinburgh was the starting-point of the survey movement in England (*sic*).

"Someone else might volunteer that Geddes had spent the better part of the last ten years in India and Palestine surveying and planning and replanning some fifty cities, and laying the foundations for the Universities of Jerusalem and Hyderabad, for Tagore's college at Santeniketon and for numerous temples and gardens. Even the physicist would have a word: he would remember Geddes as the man who anticipated Ostwald and Frederick Soddy in applying the concept of energy to the social sciences, and as the biographer of the great experimental physicist, Sir Jagadis Bose.

"We have not yet exhausted the man. The instructor in dramatics - if for the sake of convenience we may include him in this impossibly mixed group - would perhaps know that Geddes was one of the principal revivers of the masque and the pageant; while the librarian might speak a little resentfully of this Patrick Geddes who, in collaboration with Paul Otlet, the founder of the International Institute of Bibliography at Brussels, desired to substitute a rational principle of classification for the ten arbitrary categories of the Dewey decimal system, or the endless and even more arbitrary categories of the British Museum! The professor of philosophy and logic would probably be the only member of our group who had never even heard of Geddes's name; and he would wince with scepticism if I told him that, extraordinary as is the range and intensity of Geddes's thought in the fields we have been glancing at, it is as a rigorous systematic thinker, comparable to Leibnitz, Aristotle or Pythagoras, that Geddes will probably be known one day."

That day has not yet arrived and the claim is a big one; but the picture of the man as seen by Mumford who, self-confessedly, described his classic books as a life-long systematisation of Geddes's thought, cannot be treated lightly.

Mumford went on to come closer to his work in Britain as follows: "I have briefly sketched in the outward and visible results of Geddes's three-score and ten years of unceasing activity; and yet it is only a beginning. In the cupboards of the Sociological Society's headquarters in an old Victorian house in Pimlico, and in numerous rooms in the Outlook Tower at Edinburgh are boxes and bales that are filled, as it were, with the debris of Geddes's thought. There is something in the quantitative total of these notes and lectures which means more than figures can convey: these endless heaps of notations and diagrams, here complete, there but suggestive scraps, are witness to a constant fury of thought . . ."[1]

And, finally, he describes the man himself as he saw him in the Outlook Tower: "Drop in, and behold a wiry little man, with a bushy, reddish beard and a bulging forehead, carefully folding and refolding a piece of paper to serve as a diagram - a method which grew out of a period of blindness at the very outset of his career. A rapid flow of words strains through the beard in a sort of muffled soliloquy; the eyes fill with pucklike humour or with grave pity . . . and if the talk turns to the imbecility of the cockney or the stupidity of the bureaucrat or the helpless mechanisation of the modern world or the rendering unto Caesar of the things that are Caesar's and also of the things that are God's, both the humour and the pity may disappear from those grey eyes, and they will be filled instead with a red berserker rage which kindles momentarily into a memorable phrase or an epigram."

His old colleague and friend Professor H.J. Fleure, may have reflected the basic reason for this latter mood of Geddes when he said: "He was led by a vivid interest in mankind in general to make a more biological approach than was common in his youth when man was so often treated on the one hand as a unique creation and on the other as a profit-making machine."

---

1) Today, the Outlook Tower houses an Edinburgh University group which is combing systematically through "the debris. . ."

There is no simplification of the extraordinary Geddes pilgrimage through the world of ideas but, in one very important sense, Geddes's direction in thought and action from his earliest formal studies under Huxley in Biology (if anything that Geddes did was formal, either in education or administration!) led him into the social scene through his observation of the growing problems of what he named the Industrial Age - the first widespread essay by man in Technics, the Machine. And here he made the distinction through the use of new words he coined (because new wine requires new bottles). His distinction between Palaeotechnic and Neotechnic was the relation between primitive Technics and the next, somewhat more elaborate stage - principally the use of electricity. It was essentially around the potential of the new sources and usages of energy that his whole thought and work of one kind or another revolved.

In doing so Geddes gave up what, to the normal academic or scientist is the primary thing - reputation and the esteem of their peers. In his earlier days he was seriously considered a theorising genius in biology and even regarded as a potential successor to Darwin and Huxley. In collaboration with J. Arthur Thomson, once his pupil - and his life-long friend - he wrote the book *Evolution of Sex* regarded then as an original and brilliant contribution to the science of Biology. Amelia Defries in her book *The Interpreter Geddes* mentions a dinner in 1923 in Le Play House, London which was held in honour of Geddes ". . . Sir John Cockburn, who presided, said that it might surprise Professor Geddes to hear that he was one of the causes of the Womens Suffrage Movement! For, he explained, it was after reading *The Evolution of Sex* and being armed by it in his youth, that he went to Australia and there fought till women had votes. So the fight, which was afterwards taken up in London, and won there, too, a good while later, owed much to the Australians and, before them, therefore, to *The Evolution of Sex*."

Later, in 1931, their joint book on *Life and Evolution*, a comprehensive scientific publication of a major order (*see quotations on Evolution Theory in* APPENDIX I), expressed their general thesis that evolution was not necessarily the result of a "Gladiatorial Combat" - "nature red in tooth and claw", the belief so strongly expressed by Huxley - but showed more evidence of a natural sense of co-operation which was the more important cause of the ascent of Mankind to what Hamlet, in one of his great

6

soliloquies, called the "paragon of animals". The effect of this on those to whom the "kill or die" philosophy meant, at the worst, despair; and, at the best, an individual religious conviction to the contrary (although badly shaken) was very great. Planning, the exercise of foresight, presupposes hope; without such a life-giving belief the idea of purposefully planning, and working towards a better, less socially cruel, society was fatally flawed. It was to accept the literal truth of the Garden of Eden - the irredeemability of man in this world.

Geddes's work in biology, therefore, was a study which supported (and, he would say, should precede) his ideas on the improvement of human society; and his scientific research and discipline were the foundation of his life-long efforts to bring orderly categorisation to the analysis, and subsequent synthesis of the planning of man's proper and happy place in this world's environment. His celebrated *thinking machine*, therefore, the diagrams on which he spent so much of his time, were the natural outcome of the scientist matching his vision with his intellect. He constructed and used them to demonstrate possible modes of bridging the widening gap due to increasing specialisation and, so frequently, consequent introversion. Indeed, his two main teaching devices were the *thinking machine*, itself, and the diagram of what he called *The Valley Section*. Essentially the latter demonstrated a longitudinal section of landscape along a whole river valley from the hills to the sea; and covered the human occupations that were naturally to be found, from the shepherd to those in the big industrial city on the estuary where the river met the sea.

There can be much to dispute about in his words and actions; interpretations of his motives and aims can vary. But there can hardly be any dispute about his originality, his genius for turning familiar things and ideas around to demonstrate a quite new view which caught the breath. "Truth", he said, "is diamond shaped" - and he himself a diamond brilliantly reflecting from many facets.

The effect that Geddes had on me as a practising "planner" over the latter part of my career was substantial; and particularly the conviction that we should be moving out of Geddes's "Palaeotechnic Era" towards the kind of inter-disciplinary thinking and administration necessary for humanely dealing with the "Neotechnic Era".

But when I stood in Buchanan Street that night in 1932 these Geddesian neologisms were both literally and figuratively Greek to me although, in the humblest way as a civil engineering apprentice, I was then embarking on a life of creating and recreating environment - in, as it happened, the Housing Department of the then Corporation of Glasgow.

MY APPRENTICESHIP

I began my apprenticeship in the late 1920s when the great housing drive was just beginning on the basis of the post First World War Housing Acts. Even then, no more than a boy, I had vague apprehensions about the kind of environment that was being built. My feelings were affected, if not then my intellect, by the massacre of trees, hedges, lanes, streams and all the detail of landscape which people had come to value, and ramble over, in the vicinity of Glasgow - most of it very lovely. I remember one such housing site, in particular, on Glasgow's eastern boundary. In the late 1920s, this heavily wooded site was completely cleared of fine mature trees by means of a device named an "Australian Tree Puller" which, using the bigger trees as anchors, winched all the trees around them out by their very roots. The anchor trees were then felled by normal methods. One of my younger colleagues described what was left as the "smell of death"; from the rest of my colleagues there was a reaction of gusto at the efficient operation of this mechanical device. But it was the habit of the time; even little hillocks were flattened and a housing site, in the Scottish technical term, became a "cloured" site without shape or personality.

I remember only one of the younger engineers commenting adversely on the mechanical layouts then being planned. Later on, much later, I began to appreciate how very little was known in that crucially important Housing Department of the kind of thinking represented by Geddes and such peers as he had - and even of the manifestly more imaginative housing being created elsewhere, mostly abroad. Certainly, if anything of that sort were known it did not, at that time, filter down to the young people like myself who would be carrying on the work during the next generation.

So my apprenticeship drew to an end after a short spell in the City's Town Planning Department transferring on to Housing Department maps a general "planning map" of Glasgow which showed simply the very broad "zoning" of general land use over the four unbuilt quadrants of the city - all this presumably in terms of the 1925 Housing and Planning Act. The Planning Department had four men on its staff, all unqualified, without any specific background training - not in the slightest degree unusual - and this two years before the death of Geddes. But I still had not heard of Patrick Geddes, only of his namesake, Eric Campbell Geddes, he of the "Geddes Axe" and the 1930s retrenchment, which was to cut off my job along with many others as the 1929 crash led to the great Depression of that period.

In retrospect however, there were glimmerings of understanding in me of what Geddes was talking and writing about - but reaching me through other writers. How much it was he who affected the others (if at all) is now almost impossible to know. Miss Defries records a question she put to Geddes on the source of ideas: "Geddes; 'Are my ideas unique? I should hope not! They are in the air, say rather in the nature of the things as they are moving!'; 'But', I said, 'Why don't you write more?' Geddes; 'I am not an individualist, dying to patent ideas, but a teacher, trying to pass them on', he replied."

Philip Boardman, one of his later students at Montpellier, has recorded the same picture: "He consistently disclaimed priority or originality for the contributions in either the natural or the social spheres. 'Nobody has ideas of his own - we scientists do not take out patents in ideas', he said, or 'one should as soon sell one's children as one's ideas. In science, if you have an idea worth anything, you give it to the world.'"

And so it was that, particularly during my period of unemployment, I brought together a series of impressions from other reading. This was actually helped by the "leisure" forced upon me; and which, between looking for any kind of job, I used in wandering for days in the hill-country north of Glasgow and over the Highland line. I could stand on the Conic Hill above Balmaha on Loch Lomond, whose summit lay precisely on the great Highland Boundary Fault, and from there look south to the industrial lowlands of Scotland and north to thousands of square miles of high mountain country in which existed the legendary "Highland Problem", then always printed in capital letters - and which I had, over 30 years later, to deal with as the first Chairman of the Highlands and Islands Development Board.

My work, my training, my studies in the "Tech", my growing knowledge of geology (a favourite subject) and a feel for country, my walking and sleeping, all seasons, in caves and woods or on the beaches of Loch Lomond brought home to me the interconnection of Place, Work and Folk. I placed Palaeotechnic Glasgow against what was then almost the "original" Loch Lomond, so beautiful, so unspoiled, and so much an example of ecological balance. The Conic Hill, I later realised, was my equivalent of Geddes's Kinnoul Hill above Perth - where he, as a boy, had had the first overall understanding of the interconnections of country, people and work.

So, too, came together the flashes of understanding from books read outside my technical studies, . . . although it was much later that I came to the surprising conclusion that I had actually received more from them than from the then relatively small pile of strictly town-planning books I later had to read methodically for examination purposes, so relatively narrow and simple-minded. Here I am comforted and amused by Geddes's contempt for conventional education in general; I quote from his "Memo to Successors" (1930): "the would-be educationalist (coldly and dully, hence stupidly) tries to impress these high products [of the greatest minds of the past] upon his pupil's everyday feelings, consequently education is turned to instruction and this tested by memory-education, so with result of all these - as COPY, as CRAM, as JAW."

I was led as a youth, in fact, to wider (and connected) views through a certain number of vivid quasi-social novels by authors such as Jack London and H.G. Wells. Jack London, an American, overlapped Geddes's life; he wrote of the fast-changing urban and rural social scenes on the west coast of the U.S., including industrial trouble and violence. He understood industrial working-class people in a way which does not sufficiently emerge in Geddes's writing, or indeed, in British literature of the time. He wrote of the dawn of understanding in himself when, as he put it, he "opened the books" as an ignorant seaman - all this in his semi-autobiographical novel *Martin Eden*. In it, too, he describes the impact on him of Herbert Spencer's *First Principles*. Spencer, of course, had a great effect on Geddes early on, although he was strongly warned against him by Huxley, who disagreed with Spencer's much more humanistic view of nature.

It is significant that Patrick Geddes and Jack London (at first sight such incompatible figures) should each have been so affected by Spencer's synthesis. I quote from *Martin Eden*, London's

11

autobiographical novel: "what in a way most profoundly impressed Martin was the correlation of knowledge . . . all things were related to all other things from the furthermost stars in the waste of space to the myriads of atoms in the grains of sand under one's foot . . . He drew up lists of the most incongruous things, and was unhappy until he succeeded in establishing kinship between them all - kinship between love, poetry, earthquakes, fire, rattlesnakes, rainbows, precious gems, monstrosities, sunsets, the roaring of lions, illuminating gas, cannibalism, beauty, murders, levers and fulcrums and tobacco . . . And the more he knew, the more passionately he admired the universe and life and his own life in the midst of it all."

Another writer was H.G. Wells whose social and "science-fiction" novels were so often criticised by the purely literary critics. Again, in my youth, his scenarios of the extremes of high or low-density future urban living were played out before me in these novels - vividly, utopias or monstrosities. His descriptions of the unplanned growth of London, and the seedy consequences, were fascinating. And some of his characters were often involved in a search for the kind of education that would fit themselves and their children, essentially, for Geddes's Neotechnic era, e.g. as in *Joan & Peter*.

Another of his novels, *World Set Free*, dealt with the grim consequences of a world-wide nuclear war; and the setting up of a world organisation to rebuild a new society. It was dedicated to Frederick Soddy's *Interpretation of Radium*; and - hard to believe - was conceived by Wells in 1913 and published in 1914, just before World War One. It describes the organisation at Brissago in Italy as follows: "As the Brissago council came to realise that what it had supposed to be temporary camps of refugees were rapidly developing into great towns of a new type and that it was remoulding the world in spite of itself, it decided to place the work of redistributing the non-agricultural population in the hands of a compacter and better qualified special committee. That committee is now, far more than the council or any other of its delegated committees, the active government of the world. Developed from an almost invisible germ of 'town planning' that came obscurely into existence in Europe or America . . . somewhere in the closing decades of the nineteenth century, its work, the continual active planning and replanning of the world as a place of human habitation, is now, so to speak, the collective material activity of the race . . ."

Later, of course, I learned that Wells and Geddes had had many contacts, largely in the fields of energy and sociology, but were temperamentally different. A few amusing quotations at this point show that they were eventually on the same tack. H.G. Wells - then a young journalist - in a review of the first (Spring) edition of the *Evergreen* - edited by Geddes: "it's bad from cover to cover and even the covers are bad . . ." Geddes about Wells (c1905): ". . . an intellectual cockney." But 24 years later in a letter to Wells (1929) Geddes wrote: "you seem to be doing the like implicitly, alike in tales and in social thought: so is there not beginning to appear some field for co-operations . . . We have each worked mainly alone, but it now seems to me that we have come so definitely to kindred results and methods that it would be of real interest and use if we could now talk this over."

There is no record that they ever did; and Wells, for all his brilliance, foresight and imaginative power, was a cockney, in the sense of the locus of so many of his novels and of his sometimes irritating attitude to those who did not live in South-East England; Wells trained, too, under Huxley and his attitude to some of his fellow students is illuminating when he described them as having "the pale, clenched minds of the Northerner"!

Jack London died in 1916, 16 years before Geddes. Wells and Geddes both studied biology under Huxley in London. All their lives overlapped. The same seeds fell upon them all; it was a period in which a wider kind of thinking was slowly developing throughout certain sections of western civilisation principally, perhaps, because of the more frightening aspects of the swiftly-moving Industrial Revolution. Indeed, his colleagues and friends made frequent reference to him as a sower of seed. Professor H.J. Fleure, put it concisely: "Seed was cast on many soils and several of the crops that have grown therefrom, under other men's detailed care, are not connected in most people's minds with the sower . . . He was a catalyst of the mind, a pilgrim-apostle."

All this, then, I was aware of, and affected by, 15 to 20 years before I specifically heard of Geddes and his work; and my rather sad forays over the mountains as an unemployed young man brought together in my mind, at first vaguely and slowly, the terrible blunders which had been made during the Industrial

Revolution ending in the degradation of people and their immensely greater power to destroy each other and their environment. And, somewhat later, I began to appreciate the financial cost of the errors; the spending by society of so much of its treasure, so many billions of pounds paid by subsequent generations, in often miscalculated efforts to rectify the damage. As my term of unemployment came towards an end in 1933, Geddes had died just a year before, and the Town and Country Planning Act of 1932 had just come into operation - the first piece of serious legislation in Britain to deal with planning an improved future, if only in the most limited physical way.

Two years after the new Planning Act came into operation, I was working as a civil engineer in the employ of Renfrew County Council near Glasgow. I had been asked to deal with a road construction between a village housing estate and a main road. On the necessary line of this connection there were three magnificent oak trees. I remembered the massacre of trees in Glasgow; and in designing the road I split it into two carriageways, one on either side of the three oaks, thereby preserving them. I was regarded (genially) by my colleagues as an eccentric for doing so. One tends to forget just how difficult it was to do such a simple, sensitive little thing. No one seemed to think that "planning" under that pioneer Act had anything to do with such "trivial" matters.

As time went on, I became more and more involved in the 1932 Act (itself an outcome of the work of Geddes and others). A minute "planning" section (three of us, all "unqualified" as planners) was set up within the County Engineer's Department and I was asked to take it on as a primary occupation. Its main problem was to bring some order into the current big extensions on the edges of Glasgow by private housing, largely for middle-class people then beginning to move out in large numbers from the city - who, of course, were voting with their feet against the growing central muddle. But it was impossible to make enough provision for all the necessary public land-uses, for the preservation of woodland areas and hedges and so on, without paying compensation to the owners of the land, and/or the private builders. The Act had severe limitations and produced a kind of environmental aridity. Looking back, one is saddened by the difference between what was actually happening on the surface of the earth and what, by then, *should* have been happening. The

14

comparison between it and the vision and sophisticated thought of Geddes was disquieting; but, at least, some kind of discipline and thought was being exerted. And one has to note that there were at that time less than half-a-dozen "qualified" planners in the whole of Scotland.

But I still knew nothing of Geddes; and was indeed quite inadequately trained (as was my office in its administration) to get anywhere near the desiderata. All this is no particular criticism of that local authority which had, indeed, taken the Act more seriously than the great majority of its contemporaries and was actually regarded as a leader in the field.

The Act was inadequate, and so were we. Most of the people who were involved in those early days in planning were engineers, architects and surveyors. Regrettably, those not so good in their professions were sometimes pushed - or escaped - sideways into this particular field. There were less than a handful of planning schools in Britain; and they were largely designed to give a civic-design polish to architects. Over all the barren ideology of the time there brooded this extraordinary figure of Geddes - truly a great gulf.

Long afterwards, in the early 1950s, I was asked by an able civil service administrator for a list of town-planning books that might give him a clearer idea of what planning should be about. Even then I was depressed - and rather ashamed - in presenting him with the relatively meagre and simplistic handful then available; yet by that time there was the whole power of the 1947 Planning Act to administer, and this outstanding and highly-educated man was one of those who had been placed in the government planning machine to do so.

THE CLYDE VALLEY REGIONAL PLAN

The time came, however, when I became aware of Geddes and his work in a very pointed, yet comprehensive way, through being appointed to work on the Clyde Valley Plan between 1944 and 1946. The whole thing then came together for me.

Before the Second World War ended, when it was clearly moving towards the predominance of the Allies in all fields, post-war reconstruction plans were beginning to be taken seriously and put in hand. Behind them stood the Barlow Commission Report published in 1940 - and shelved, when Britain was intent on other more immediately pressing matters. It was entitled *The Distribution of the Industrial Population* and addressed itself chiefly to the pressing problems of the million-mark conurbations, the latter word, incidentally, having been coined by Geddes, one of his many neologisms; and first officially used in the post-war Census of 1951.

This was a fundamental Report which was discussed more intensively as the war came to its final stages. Indeed, it was the major Report around which other important Reports revolved - the Reith Report on New Towns; the Uthwatt Report on Compensation and Betterment (on land values); the National Parks Reports, one for England and Wales, the other for Scotland; and the Scott Report on Land Utilisation in Rural Areas dealing with countryside administration. The Barlow report pointed to the consequent need for decentralisation and much more powerful planning legislation.

All these reflected the usual desire for reform after a great war. All of them had a greater or lesser effect on the post-war planning and reconstruction of this country. One or two, like the New Towns Report, have had major, solid and successful effects. Finally, therefore, there was the passing of the most powerful planning legislation ever enacted up to that time in this country, the Town and Country Planning Act, 1947, which came into effect in July 1948.

It is difficult to convey today the power of this focus on replanning our society; this urge to renovate and reconstruct on more pleasant and equitable lines; and on a basis of more participation by the folk of the country themselves.

It was this universal desire which led the then Secretary of State for Scotland, Mr Tom Johnston, to convene a meeting of the 18 local authorities in Clydeside; and to persuade them to set up a regional planning advisory committee to make proposals for reconstruction through the agency of a regional plan. In 1944 the Clyde Valley Regional Planning Advisory Committee was set up. It appointed as its Consultant, Professor Sir Patrick Abercrombie; and thereafter a staff of professionals.

Abercrombie was just bringing to completion the Greater London Plan (published 1945); he had a world reputation and, very important, in him was the first real connection with Geddes in serious large-scale practice, because he had known Geddes personally and had worked with him. But, curiously enough, he never at any time talked to us about him in staff discussions. Indeed, it was eight years after the plan was completed that I heard him describe his connections with Geddes at the centenary of his birth at a conference in the Outlook Tower, Edinburgh in 1954.

Nevertheless, but vaguely, certain discussions took place within the staff; one became aware that our Plan offered a real possibility of following the Geddesian principles of survey, analysis and plan. At 33 years of age, therefore, I was confronted by him and started to study material written by, and about, him. It was perhaps as well that I was reasonably mature and had had some experience of planning work in local government - where the realities of politics, public administration and legislation could not be avoided; but where, too, the need for a regional approach to local problems had become more and more obvious.

At the beginning of work on the Plan, a small number of individuals were asked to come and talk to us, people who had knowledge of major urban and rural studies. Arthur, the son of Patrick Geddes, was the first of that few. He outlined what he thought we should look for and bring together in our initial survey in terms of his father's vision. But Arthur, who later became a good and sensitive friend of mine, left me with a hazy feeling that although the *principles* enunciated were true and good, they somehow did not fit a huge "Palaeotechnic" city-cluster like Clydeside. Perhaps they didn't fit the people - the largely working class population of a modern manufacturing conurbation. Later -

17

and now - I reflect on the fact (so far as I have studied the matter) that Geddes said little about Clydeside or the Highlands - and seldom visited either of them. Yet they were - they are - the two really outstanding problems of Scotland at either end of the range, although connected socially by migration and blood. It has occurred to me that perhaps a cardinal image of Scotland in the mind of Geddes was the old pre-industrial population grouping - the Lothians and up the Vale of Strathmore; and Edinburgh, after all, has more of the atmosphere of a fine large country town than of a 19th century industrial town or city as we now know it in the United Kingdom. But this is conjecture though certainly based on real thought and close reading. The Edinburgh slums in which Geddes worked with his wife Anna were not like those of Clydeside either in scale or kind; in a sense, they were like a laboratory sample surrounded by aseptic bourgeois material and therefore much more easy to define, study, - and, perhaps, patronise.

The outstanding visitor was Frank Fraser Darling (later Sir Frank) who came to talk about national and regional parks and the handling of countryside problems in general. He was then involved in the West Highland Survey and on the Scottish National Parks Survey Committee. Later, within 2 or 3 years, I was to collaborate with him on National Park work and on his West Highland Survey. I think, above all those contemporaries who came to talk to our pioneer organisation, he was the most thoughtful and had the widest range of questions about man and his environment. He too, of course, was a biologist and later became a world-famous "conservationist". The fact is that the *approach* of Arthur Geddes and Frank Darling made such planning textbooks as existed (most of them primarily a branch of architecture, and affected by the physical determinism of the drawing-board) almost derisory in the face of the problems to be tackled. Or, if they dealt with the legalities of the Planning Acts, they were arid in themselves unless informed by a spirit and inspiration of the wider kind.

One does not wish to make too much of this in detail but bigger questions of principle were raised in our minds - principles difficult to quantify in the simpler terms of ordinary numeracy. Today, in parenthesis, our contemporary Government in their desire to toughen up the country (no longer imperial) which has become slack and has perhaps too high expectations, talk about "living within our means". But what would Geddes have meant by "means" or by "live"? And about backing a competitive society, dominated by selling and marketing, which through commercial television and other media, forces people to want, and spend, more than their real needs require - and fuel the constant demand for higher wages? Geddes said compelling things about this, too, (before television) and addressed them to the "cinema people" of his day: and one such discussion is recorded in the first biography of Geddes by Amelia Defries (1927). (*See* APPENDIX I.)

So, with much internal discussion, even of this kind, the Clyde Valley Plan proceeded through its two years of preparation and everything gradually fell into a pattern of thought and action which was of the essence of the thing that Geddes had preached; it was as though, through a process of osmosis, the Geddesian philosophy was inherent in the growth of the plan itself.

All the elements were there. The Clyde Valley Plan was the first really big opportunity in Scotland (big in terms of people and problems) to attempt to put into practice his general principles of regional survey, analysis and synthesis; to bring together different knowledges and disciplines; to declare the basis of action; and to focus on the kind of changes and renewals required to bring that great area of 19th century destruction to something like a more natural and humane order.

Further, an important move was made into the principle of participation. We gathered together all the people dealing with countryside recreation, outdoor sports and natural history, and asked them to bring together a group to produce a survey of their needs and desires. This was convened by an amateur naturalist, an ex-shipwright from Clydeside. They produced a remarkable report and we incorporated it in our wider socio-economic regional plan. This, though on the edge of the major urban problems, was truly a pioneer effort, which foreshadowed much of the participation movement of the 1970s.

When the final illustrated edition of the Clyde Valley Regional Plan was published, Sir Frederick Osborn - that courageous and literate pioneer who then headed the Town and Country Planning Association[1] - said this in a review in *The Spectator* of January 27,

---

1) A biography of Osborn entitled *F.J.O., Practical Idealist* by Arnold

1950: ". . . More dramatically than any other Region, the Clyde symbolises what man can do with the earth for good and ill . . . Vaguely we all have the picture in our minds. This superb report - the masterpiece of the Abercrombie series - confirms it, yet transforms it by filling it out with a wealth of living detail. It is at once a geography of the region, a history of its development, an analysis of its economy, the study of the ways and work of its people, an appreciation of its beauties and uglinesses and a philosophy of physical planning. The diverse information brought together is so well digested, and the writing and editing so good, that the book can be read right through with unflagging interest. It is magnificently illustrated. I am tempted to say that it would come into the class of fine literature but for the fact that it displays statistical sense as well as sensitivity. To read this book is to come nearer to understanding the vast and changing complex of the Clyde Valley than would have been possible by years of study before this modern type of planning survey emerged."

The Clyde Valley Plan was one of the two regional plans in Scotland launched just after the war; the other was the Central and South East Regional Plan (covering the Lothians and the Eastern Border Country) and there was close collaboration between the two regional planning teams covering most of the central belt of Scotland; I remember vividly our frequent inter-office discussions and our successful handling of overlaps.

In some ways the Central and South East plan stood closer to the Geddesian approach because of the consultant who headed it - Sir Frank Mears. He was the son-in-law of Patrick Geddes and his collaborator in various past projects ranging from the Edinburgh Zoo to the University of Jerusalem. For certain reasons, including Sir Frank's presence and attitudes, his staff were more overtly conscious of the Geddes philosophy. The Tweed Basin section of the final report is, I think, very Geddesian; here is something like Geddes's famous teaching examples, the "Valley Section", presented in reality in one of the great river valleys of Scotland.

As I have said, such a loose-texture region with serious rural problems was probably closer to the Scottish scene in Geddes's

---

Whittick was published by the T.C.P.A. in 1987.

mind; and one wonders how he might have tackled the massive Industrial Revolution character of the Clyde Valley Region in the real process of regional planning, as one wonders about his unwillingness to accept and master the distortions created by the more serious metropolitan political realities - and of the consequent legislation with all its dangers of aridity.

Unquestionably, however, the same principles were applied, more or less consciously, by the Clyde Valley Team. In the event, the Clyde Valley Plan was accepted as a major guide by central government in Scotland; and some of its staff was brought into St. Andrew's House to further that important final step in the process, action on the ground.[1]

---

1) Geddes's contention in this respect was very clear; one of his often-quoted comments is that *"planning without action is simply playing into the puzzles of the maze."*

THE SCOTTISH OFFICE

In March 1946 I entered the employment of the then Department of Health for Scotland. This Department covered the central government administration of health, housing and town & country planning. It will be appreciated that the post-war Welfare State atmosphere, politically and administratively, put a particular emphasis on health and housing and this was reflected in the staffing and power of these sections. New planning legislation was being considered and the Town and Country Planning (Scotland) Act 1947 became law in July 1948. Ad interim, administration proceeded in a tentative way under the 1932 Act which had serious limitations.

Seen against the preliminary edition of the plan published in March 1946[1] - a plan which could be said to combine Geddes's Valley Section approach to this great industrial valley with his idea of synthesis through the Place, Work, Folk triad - even the new planning Act of 1947 was soon seen to be inadequate. Even less did the Act fit the unique character of the Highland and Islands region which, in an area of one-sixth of the land-surface of the United Kingdom, had a population of less than 300,000. It was completely different in scale and kind from any other region of the United Kingdom yet had a disproportionate effect on Scottish thinking and dissatisfaction. Planning, in any real sense, was in the hands of the Department of Agriculture for Scotland in an area where the social-economic pattern was almost wholly that of the crofting system, a system of small-scale subsistence agriculture with an ethos (and language, in many areas) of a unique kind.

---

1) As the authorities in the Regional Advisory Committee (especially the City of Glasgow) realised the planning and administrative implications they were loath to put up the money for the fully-illustrated Edition, and it was proofed, designed and paid for by the Scottish Office. It was published in 1949 by H.M. Stationery Office.

In the wider sphere the Act was not really shaped to fit Scotland. There was, at that time, a joke current in the corridors of St. Andrews House, the headquarters of Scottish government administration: "How many times today have you changed 'Minister of Town and Country Planning' to 'Secretary of State for Scotland?'." Indeed, in 1948, I found myself in real trouble as a fledgling civil servant. I had been asked, as the chairman of the Scottish Branch of the Town Planning Institute, to give a talk in Glasgow to the Highland Development League on the Act as it might affect the Highlands and its development. I summed up by saying that the Act was essentially designed to arbitrate in competition in land-use (but not agricultural land-use) whereas the real problem of the Highlands was to *induce* competition in land-use! I was formally carpeted for this gaffe. Sixteen years later (then Chief Planning Officer) I was about to leave the Scottish Office to take up the new Chair of Town and Regional Planning in Glasgow University. I was given a farewell party presided over by Sir Douglas Haddow, the permanent Under-Secretary of State who ended his little speech by saying that he had gone over my "black book" and found that piece of political ingenuousness among my recorded indiscretions - "but," he said, "who would disagree with Bob now!"

When I began work in the Scottish Office as one of its three Regional Planning Officers it was on the basis of a decision much later described in a paper to the Royal Town Planning Institute in London (1968) by J.H. McGuinness, then an Under-Secretary in the Scottish Development Department; this decision was to bring some of the Clyde Valley Plan staff into the Scottish Office, after publication of the plan, to interpret and further its recommendations. I was invited to take on one of the regional planning officer posts - and, since it was vacant, that for the North Region - presumably temporarily. So, in 1946, I found myself faced with the "Highland Problem", regarded as practically insoluble, and therefore an incubus to be endured and kept quiet by a succession of small and disconnected measures.

That was the general background and the very small professional planning group of North Region in 1946 had many discussions on how it could make a more fundamental planning approach to such a region. As it happened, the occasion arose that year in connection with the Highland peninsula of Applecross in Wester Ross - a very isolated mountainous area connected to the tortuous

West-coast road system by a narrow, dangerous road rising in a series of very acute bends to nearly 2,000 feet above sea-level. This really fearsome road was frequently blocked by snow in spring and winter and the people of Applecross had no other connection with the mainland than a small boat connection with the Macbrayne Steamer to Skye - but this only possible in calm weather. They, for a time, made their genuine grievance and acute sense of isolation into a *cause celebre*;[1] and we thought the whole business deserved a trial run in Highland regional survey technique.

On that survey trip in May 1946, we walked nearly 40 miles in all; I, from Tornapress, on a rough mountain track past the ruined and deserted township of Uags to Toscaig. I had an Abney level with me to give some idea of the gradients of a possible vehicular road round the southern end of the peninsula; but I had to rule out the practical possibility of this 12-mile section. Round the 20-miles of the north end we walked on sections of the track from Applecross village to Shieldaig, that charming village on the coastal road. We stopped at every minute crofting township and talked eventually to every crofter gathering information on work, population by families - and personal views.

The Report eventually covered population, its movements and work; agricultural activities from the interviews and such statistics as were available in the Scottish Department of Agriculture and Fisheries; possible afforestation areas, tourism etc; and even the working-out of a small community hydro-electric scheme based on a loch 1,000 feet up.

The outcome of that trip to Applecross was a report of 40,000 words. With all its faults, it could be said to be the kind of rambling synthesis which Geddes might have written - but in more conventional English! The whole professional planning staff of North Region produced it - three of us - one a Rome Scholar in Architecture (a qualified planner) who had been educated in the Edinburgh College of Art where he had heard of Geddes through his lecturer, Sir Frank Mears, Geddes's son-in-law. One was a geographer educated in Edinburgh University, whose lecturers

---

1) Indeed, the subject of a book by Eric Linklater, and a very amusing film: *Laxdale Hall.*

included Geddes's son, Dr. Arthur Geddes.[1] It was the geographer-planner who wrote the Report, and it was he who had most methodically absorbed the ethos of Patrick Geddes.

This total disappearance of the professional planning staff for a week bothered the junior administrative staff who complained that no one was there for that period to deal with the routine of change of use cases. I conveyed the Report to the Assistant Secretary dealing with planning - the administrator in the conventional British Civil Service sense and a man of first class intellect. He read it and, in discussion later, summed up his view, ". . . I'm afraid it simply spells out to me the bankruptcy of the whole Highland development idea." To him, seen against the immensely greater problems of planning post-war reconstruction in a heavily-urbanised country, it must have seemed a misuse of the proverbial sledge-hammer. I understood, but was clear enough in my own mind that this trial run was justifiable and that each region must have the kind of handling that suited it from the micro to the macro-textural.

There were other strands in the web of our work that made for more fruitful reports. One was the connection with the West Highland Survey which had its modest headquarters at Strontian, 70 miles due south of Applecross, and a much greater distance by road in that deeply-indented and mountainous coastline. This comprehensive survey effort was set up and financed by the Scottish Office through the Department of Agriculture and Fisheries. It was headed by Frank Fraser Darling, later to develop a world reputation in the conservation movement.

We had met earlier in connection with the National Park surveys and both of us were still serving on the Scottish National Park Committee, then moving up to its final Report published in 1947. There was a division of opinion on the Committee which was never contentious; but two or three of us strongly felt that care was needed in our recommendations to emphasise that national parks must not be a take-over bid by those who were dominated by the idea of Parks primarily as wild-life reserves, a kind of public version of the more restrictive deer-forest proprietors. Our view, in

---

1) Respectively A.B. Wylie and F.D.N. Spaven.

essence, was that the Highlander in the past had been exploited (and expropriated) for trees, for sheep, for deer - and now for scenery. This time, he should be in on the business and, bluntly, should share more clearly in the employment and the decision-making.

The outcome of this was the preparation of a kind of minority report entitled the Glen Affric Addendum which was, in effect, a comprehensive plan for an area of the Highlands picked out by the preceding National Parks Survey committee as one of the five or six of outstanding scenic value. Further, the newly-created North of Scotland Hydro-electric Board was well advanced in its planning and had picked out the Glen Affric area for one of its biggest developments.

The plan therefore, had to be of synthesis demonstrating a possible bringing together of tourism, agriculture, flood control (via design of the Hydro-electric works) and therefore more (and more reliable) wintering for the hill stock on the low valley ground - and finally, improved hill agriculture with the right kind of forestry. Those elements were visualised which would be expected from national park use - improved hill tracks, rough shelters and hostel and hotel accommodation, all reflecting more local employment. In effect it was a sketch of a possible rural regional plan.

The West Highland Survey too, was in its preliminary stages and my earlier visits to Fraser Darling at Strontian led to many discussions well into the night on more integrated approaches to Highland rehabilitation and development. One such outcome was an agreement with the Scottish Agricultural Organisation Society to collaborate on a survey of the Island of Coll. Such small Hebridean Islands posed a special problem in their isolation, dependence on steamer services, the quality of piers at which they could berth and, of course, their sometimes very difficult weather conditions.

By 1948, therefore, in collaboration and discussion with the local people of the Island a comprehensive report was produced. Thirty-seven years later (in 1985), when I returned to Coll on a survey of Island ferry services as Chairman of the Consultative Council to HIDB, I found that the Report was very much remembered; had been partly implemented - and was genuinely valued.

Those two or three years, therefore, constituted for me an important period in my professional life; I gained, close up, a deeper understanding of the "Highland Problem" which stood me in good stead when, much later, I found myself in Inverness as the first chairman of the newly-created Highlands and Islands Development Board. I had, in fact, been applying the Geddesian approach subconsciously, skirting the edge of statutory planning procedure!

But, by 1949, I was transferred to the industrial West Region - back to Geddes's "Palaeotechnic" Scotland. The dominant problem was Clydeside - and the Clyde Valley Plan, had just been published in a fully-illustrated format. So I came back to what was the first real impact of the recommendations of that Plan; and, above all, to the almost incredible statistics of the housing problem - and to its politics. For here, other urban slum problems were dwarfed by the outcome of the calculations of the Regional Plan's survey of Glasgow - 700,000 people compressed into 1,800 acres in and around the central city, a gross- and net-density (because there was no public or other open space) of nearly 400 persons to the acre. The 1951 Census, which for the first time included details of housing standards, established that the City's unique housing congestion was due to its having more people to the room and less rooms to the house than any other British conurbation. When it is realised that when the later multi-storey housing policy swept the country, the highest density "achieved" was about 180, the dimensions of the "overspill" consequence - even with that really inhuman solution - were enormous. Roughly put, the "overspill" amounted to a quarter of a million out of Glasgow's then total population of 1,100,000.

By 1948 I was living in Edinburgh and had become involved in the Outlook Tower Association and, for the first time, was brought in close touch with Geddes's background and written material; and also with some of his collaborators, e.g. Arthur, his son, and Sir Frank Mears, his son-in-law. Essentially, therefore, I was thinking about Geddes directly and with some real understanding when, from within the Civil Service, I had to give professional advice on the Clydeside problem to the administration.

But Geddes and his approach did not seem to fit as it did, essentially, in the Highlands. The discrepancy had something to do with scale, with way of life, with a very real degradation of

27

human standards which Geddes himself had emphasised on his
examination of the Palaeotechnic City with another set of Greek
neologisms ("Metropolis, Megalopolis, Parasitopolis
Necropolis"!). Further, there was Geddes's utter rejection of the
idea of the centralist handling of such a problem - of a government
"plan", central or local. Sociologically, he profoundly believed, the
re-creation of a better society had to begin at the level, and with
the co-operation, of the people themselves. He had a profound
distrust of the political machine. One of his biographers, much
later, made the point that he had taken "the fateful step of
ignoring political debate."[1]

What Geddes, sometimes called "The Father of Modern Town
Planning", would have thought of the Clyde Valley Plan is a matter
for a wide range of conjecture; but it stood at that time - and, I
believe, yet - as one of the best regional plans in Britain.[2] Very
certainly, his way of going about solving such problems in Indian
cities would hardly have fitted here. Boardman quotes from
Patrick Geddes in India Geddes's own account of criss-crossing on
foot an entire slum quarter that was threatened with
drawing-board "relief of congestion" until he could show by his
map of the neighbourhood how "conservative surgery" would
achieve the desired result without wholesale demolition and at a
fraction of the cost. This procedure in Glasgow would have
confronted dwellers who were politically-conscious trade
unionists and had votes and ideas of their own, right or wrong -
and elected representatives who had visions of *their* own and
wanted the best. "We're not going to be treated like second class
citizens" was a strong comment made by a Housing Committee
member at a Scottish Office-Glasgow Corporation meeting to
discuss this truly terrible problem, and to consider a rather feeble
suggestion of partial rehabilitation of the Gorbals area and the
opening-up of the ends, and landscaping between the existing
rectangular tenement blocks - which, incidentally, would have left
a still very great problem of overspill to be housed elsewhere. If

1) Helen Meller: *Patrick Geddes - Social Evolutionist and Planner*, (1990).
2) See the book *Strategic Planning in Action* by Smith and Wannop (1985)
- end of Evaluation chapter: "*Forty years later it had not been surpassed in any
case of regional or metropolitan planning in the United Kingdom.*"

the Convenor had heard of Geddes, he would probably have added that Glasgow had a Lord Provost at the top of the political tree - not a Maharajah with the British Raj behind him.

In the event most of the unavoidable overspill was housed in peripheral areas on the edge of the city - two of them of great natural and man-made beauty. The housing was built as quickly as possible with methods and materials that have caused serious problems of dampness and heat-loss since; and almost competely lacked the facilities that make the difference between a "housing scheme" and a community of work, folk and place. They are now among Glasgow's most notorious problem areas; yet, within a mile of one of them - and built in the same period - is the new town of East Kilbride, built under the New Towns Act of 1946, and originally proposed in the Clyde Valley Plan. This town is clearly a success with its own industries, its social facilities, and a remarkable number of social and cultural organisations. But it just does not fit Geddes's recipe for such a development; it emerged from central government legislation; was fought for through a major public inquiry by central government; in its early stages was steered into its present form by government officials and carried on to its completion by an appointed New Town Corporation. It was, in fact, the fruit of a generation of politics and political debate about the legislation, administration and powers needed to set it up; and many of the pioneers who pushed (and educated) the politicians on the need for such a new animal were aware of the matters that exercised the minds of men like Geddes - and some like Sir George Pepler and Sir Frederick Osborn who were aware of and knew Geddes himself and his works.

The day was to come, however, when Geddes's deeper principle of community responsibility (and knowledge) would be reflected - from the late 60s onwards - by the Housing Associations and Co-operatives; and the growth of action by young community architects, lawyers and other professionals, and the community organisations they serviced; e.g. Technical Services Agency Ltd. All this burgeoning of confidence, self-help and real knowledge by ordinary folk I saw at close quarters and in total during my chairmanship of the comprehensive Glasgow Housing Inquiry and its public hearings in 1986. It has to be emphasised, however, that the population within Glasgow's boundaries by that time had decreased by two or three hundred thousand and the housing stock involved was of a somewhat better kind; the reduction of central density had made this new approach possible - physically.

Concurrently, too, the administration of the Scottish Office from the middle-1950s onwards progressively reflected a movement towards a conjunction of those elements from different departments which had dealt with housing and planning. This took place even through the successive changes of government, Conservative and Labour, with their ups and downs of policy. More and more sophisticated approaches were made to regional surveys and strategies which became those of a wider synthesis.

The first comprehensive administrative move in the Scottish Office came with the creation of the Scottish Development Department in 1962 which brought together all planning and infrastructural services and included, for the first time, an economic advice service; it was also, of course, reflecting a growing concern for the under-privileged regions of the United Kingdom. This initial important step eventually had issue in the *White Paper on the Scottish Economy* (1966) which covered all the regions of Scotland - and in the Highland component of which the HIDB found a valuable basis for its subsequent "action-planning". This whole process was covered by J.H. McGuinness of the Scottish Office in his 1968 paper to the Royal Town Planning Institute already mentioned. In it he said: "There was a certain historical inevitability in the evolution and . . . the trend is now irreversible." At the time I felt that that was correct in the sense of a growth of a more integrated handling and approach; leaving only the questions as to how far it could be steered through the more extreme vagaries of politics and how far it would succeed in winning the understanding and co-operation of the folk affected.

As I write, however, over 20 years later, I find myself serving on an official working party on the Gorbals-Hutchesontown district of Glasgow whose notorious past is a symbolic challenge and where past errors of planning and action in the 1960s, and later, have left behind an urban desert. This time a real effort is being made to create active participation in decision-making with the folk still there. A new working vocabulary is clearly being used - and, one hopes, will be put into action all through the process. Time will tell - but at least a clear intent is visible in our discussions within a group representing all the powers which will require to work out in the open its philosophy, finance, administration - and participation.

I must not end this chapter without paying tribute to the Scottish Office. At the upper levels of administration I have to record that I met the best collection of balanced and educated minds of any organisation I have ever worked in. I only regretted that there was not then more movement for them into the fields of action and education for reasonable periods of time; and across the gap between the administrative *cadre* and its professional fellows. Finally, qua the wider question of Devolution; I am convinced that they would have been more than capable of servicing an administration more clearly and efficiently detached from Whitehall.

THE UNIVERSITY

At all times, and like all radicals of his times, Geddes put the highest importance on education; and he could be its most pungent critic, as practised. He was no friend of standard academe and his comments on its rather introverted world brought forth from him many and often-quoted broadsides. For those who depend for their ascent of the academic ladder on a clear and lengthy list of publications, such of his comments as have been recorded must be, at least, irritating, e.g. "When one crystallises his thought into print he ceases to think" — or, "When an idea is dead it is embalmed in a text-book." Bertrand Russell, in *The History of Western Civilisation*, quotes Helvetius, the 18th century French Philosopher, as having the view - as others of his school - that the principle instructors of adolescence are the forms of government and the consequent manners and customs - and this is reflected in the forms of state education. Russell's idiosyncratic summing-up of this school of thought was: "Men are born ignorant, not stupid; they are made stupid by education."

Helen Meller, an academic historian, says in her important biography of 1990: "Since the days . . . of the great Paris World Exposition of 1900 when he had turned even more away from the idea of seeking an academic milieu for working out his ideas he had pursued his work as if it was a crusade." It was, of course, in the nature of a crusade; and it is clear from a study of his life that he would have been a crusader even as a full-time professor - as have other academics in history. His professorship of Botany in Dundee was part-time and, from the conventional point of view, was undoubtedly eccentric though apparently enjoyed for its inspiration by his students; and, in recorded afterthought, quite deeply by some of his colleagues. In essence, of course, he was really in the business of *making* history.

When I moved in 1965 from the Scottish Office to Glasgow University's first chair of Planning, my first emotions were of real pride and a new freedom - the freedom to speak my mind publicly, guided and controlled only by my own knowledge, reason and feeling. But, in practice, I had never found my previous situation too bothersome, nor the new one particularly "free". The most important thing for me was really the opportunity to create, if possible, something like a new "Humanities" course in line with the challenges of a technological society, to teach, to convey to relatively mature postgraduates the essence of planning from the realities I had personally encountered - the process, rather than the plan; and to identify clearly the bridges that might be built to cross the gaps where the "disciplines" came closest to each other.

The encounter with lively students was, to me, the greatest of pleasures, and of rewards; and still is. But my hopes (and I confess my ingenuousness) could not really survive the reality of the University system, as it is, with its narrowing (and proliferation) of specialisms, when the need, somewhere, was for any sane and successful system to be based on something like the Geddesian synthesis.

THE HIGHLANDS AND ISLANDS
DEVELOPMENT BOARD

My initial entry to the University was to be short-lived. In that first year my colleagues and I were only at the beginning of our discussions on policy, the problems of interdisciplinary teaching arrangements, tentative feelers to the Royal Town Planning Institute for professional recognition etc., when a quite unexpected thing happened. I was approached by the Secretary of State to consider taking on the chairmanship of the new Highland development authority; the Bill for the Highlands and Islands Development Act was passing through its final stages in Parliament.

It was a painful and difficult decision to make; but I believed strongly that positive action could be taken about the "Highland Problem". The *White Paper on the Scottish Economy*, then being prepared, showed signs of a more positive approach to the Highlands and Islands region. Eventually, I decided to accept and the University generously gave me five years leave of absence on the understanding that I kept in touch with the setting-up of the course and periodically visited staff and students. This was a very difficult matter to carry out properly, particularly in the first two years of very high pressure and controversy about the work of the Board; however, I moved to Inverness in November 1965 and set the Board in action.

There was no precedent for the HIDB; as I said at the beginning of its life in November 1965, "we started with the paper-clips!" It was, at that time, the only regional development authority in Britain. The need for such a body had been strongly urged by many voices for decades - including the Highland Panel, an advisory group, chaired by Lord Cameron, a senior and celebrated Scottish judge.

Harold Wilson in the early 60s had promised in a political speech in Inverness that, on return to power of a Labour government, a special Highland development authority would be set up. The promise was kept in spite of strong Conservative criticism during the passage of the Bill through Parliament; indeed, the expression, "a Marxist enactment", was used. However, opposition was withdrawn as the Board's subsequent actions showed results, and thereafter was backed by subsequent governments.

This, perhaps, was because the Board was pursuing the Geddesian maxim of planning and action in parallel. Certainly, by that time, I was deeply affected by his maxim and his own record of action - and by my earlier efforts from the Scottish Office to achieve genuine contact with certain individuals in the University of Glasgow in order to collaborate particularly in economic-physical planning. Chief among these academics was a very able and young Professor of Economics, Donald Robertson, who showed real willingness to create a productive relationship and whose untimely death shortly after my return to the University was a great blow to me, personally and academically.

Later - back whole-time in the University in 1970 - I found myself facing the question from my colleagues: "Where was your plan for the Highlands?" One year after that, at the Town Planning Institute Annual Conference held in Edinburgh in May 1971, I gave a paper on the work of the Board. Under the heading "Action Planning", I dealt with that question as follows: "In the first place, the Board was wholly disinclined to take two or more years to produce a 'plan' for the Highlands and Islands. In a region of such great complexity and such a history of neglect - as the Highlander saw it - the conventional planning approach was not possible, to say the least of it. There already existed a great mass of survey material and comment. Too much, and a lot of it not to the point. One can always add, intelligently or otherwise, to such a mass; the Board chose not to. On the basis of what existed (and accepting the only generally accepted proposition from a mountain of comment - that depopulation was the central problem) the Board stated its strategy in three of four pages in its first *Annual Report*. That strategy was its first 'plan' - and its approach to action was something like this:

"1. It declared a strategy based on job-making potential.

"2. It moved as quickly as possible into 'performing a multitude of fruitful actions' under that umbrella strategy, no matter how small each individual project might be, so that the Highlander (and others) would believe that when it produced specific plans they would be acted upon - they might even work!

"3. At the same time it would start the production of plans for specific sectors of economic activity or for particular areas - e.g., fisheries, tourism, at least one bigger growth area - and move into implementation as soon as plans were completed. (In fact, plans of this sort were worked out within the first year of the Board's life, the fisheries plans within the first six months.) Other plans within the strategy would follow as seemed necessary or practicable.

"In practice, the Board's staff and tempo evolved to effect this approach. Particularly strong emphasis developed on the management side, i.e., the industrial-commercial management advice and accountancy services. Any conceivable Highland development strategy must assume a large proportion of small enterprises because of the social-economic texture of the area and because of its geography; and small commercial concerns and industries are particularly vulnerable to poor management . . ." [*And on the physical and environmental issues*] . . . "The Board worked as closely as possible with the existing local authorities. It did not attempt to interfere with their principal role as physical planning and infrastructure authorities; it adhered as tightly as possible to the economic development role for itself, but always with a strong social colour in its economic policy. It only entered the local authority field in one major operation - the commissioning of a comprehensive physical regional plan for the Inner Moray Firth which it paid for and handed over to the local authorities concerned for public discussion.[1] Essentially, therefore, whilst it always declared its strong adherence to the conservation equation, it could not itself effect that; fundamentally, it acted the part of the enlightened patron on development and would ally itself with those charged with amenity and conservation matters . . . One of the most important results was the progressive welding together of a staff which was about one-third from public service and two-thirds from the business and academic worlds. The progressive growth of a common vocabulary of power was clearly visible. This took time and evolved imperfectly but may hold much

---

1) In my initial discussions with the Convenors of the key County Councils I put it this way: *"If we are successful in pulling the economic trigger we must take some responsibility for the social and economic consequences. . . "*

of significance for regional development in the future. As for myself, I found that my actions as a quasi-political Chairman were greatly helped and clarified by the planning colour in my mental process. That, in itself, is a not unimportant final comment; it bears strongly on the question of the value of a 'planning' education for those who will have to deal with public affairs."

To finish this account of the essence of HIDB policy I return to our first "plan" for fisheries development in the Western Isles; and I recall my first attempts, via the Scottish Office, to apply some kind of planning approach to remote areas of the Highlands and Islands in 1946. Now, 20 years later, a similar exercise was carried out over the whole length of the Outer Isles from the island of Vatersay through Barra, Eriskay, South Uist, Benbecula, North Uist, Harris and Lewis, and finally ending at Stornoway - 150 miles in total; all this in winter conditions, much in darkness and poor weather. This time, however, the initial survey was carried out by the Chairman of the Board, its Secretary and the Board member for fisheries; and with the power and finance of an *ad hoc* authority. We were taking the first steps towards the implementation of our fisheries development scheme aimed at the methodical resuscitation of fishing as a primary economic activity which had practically died out after World War Two.[1]

We started in Barra and held meetings with local people and representatives in all kinds of accommodation, school and church halls - or in the open. We were greeted everywhere with a cool and wary interest as another collection of mainlanders, another set of officials of the "plus-four and deerstalker brigade" who might never be seen again.

We asked the Roman Catholic priest of Barra - the natural spokesman - how we could speak to the handful of people who lived in the last inhabited island of Vatersay on the Saturday we arrived. He told us to cross from Barra on the little ferry the next day, Sunday, and wait outside the door of the church till the inhabitants came out at the end of the 12 o'clock mass. We did,

---

1) The Board's justification of the crofting system and its need for the support of ancillary employment (e.g. fisheries) is clearly set down in its 1st Annual Report of May 1967.

and discussed their problems in the open. Two days, and a number of meetings later, we were treated to a magnificent little speech by the Chairman of North Uist District Council - the Free Church Minister - who cast scorn on tourism as one of the solutions, but strongly backed our fisheries scheme as much more likely to fit the ethos of North Uist.

We ended, after more meetings, in a little smoke-filled attic room in Stornoway, talking to the representatives of the Western Isles Crofters Union. We were faced with the distrust and disbelief of the Chairman who believed - as we knew from our first tense and heated meeting in Inverness - that the Board had been set up to destroy the crofting system. We argued with him and them. In the end the articulate and able chairman (headmaster of Shawbost junior secondary school) seemed to believe that we were in earnest about our fisheries development plan, and were able to spend money on training young crofters through training boats and skippers; and making arrangements for the entrants to buy mid-water trawlers with low-interest rate loans.

The meeting ended with the convivial drinking of whisky and the beginning of trust and acceptance. An unforgettable end to our journey. The scheme was carried out and Charles MacLeod, the headmaster - although always properly critical of the Board's policies - became a good friend as time went on. Indeed, long afterwards, and when - having left the Board - I became the Chairman of its Consultative Council in 1978 (poacher turned gamekeeper!), and found Charles serving on it, our friendship became a firm and valued one and only ended with his death. I am pretty sure that Geddes would have approved of, and enjoyed, that whole trip in 1966, method, outcome - and people.

FINAL REFLECTIONS

So then, long after his death, I (one planner) saw and was involved in action that brought me to understand in practice what Geddes had been after - the progression of thought that, as a biologist, began for him with his life-giving view of evolution, not as a gladiatorial combat but as he once said "a vast and endless mothers meeting"! He stood for the hopeful and gentler bases of life, through orderly and cooperative methods of synthesis, using his mode of thought and his "thinking machines". And then the action that should follow . . . "planning and action should not be divided" and the continuing process of analysis and synthesis by the appropriate administrative means.

Increasingly, therefore, Sir William Holford's paraphrase of the epigram about Plato at the Centennial in Edinburgh in 1954 was real to me when I heard it repeated - and not just clever: "wherever I go in my mind I meet Geddes coming back."

So my first impressions of him were vague hearsay of a remarkable man (largely because some thoughtful and sensitive men and women I had knowledge of, or had acquaintance with, thought him remarkable); ingenious; his Place-Work-Folk diagrams leading to a wider inter-connectedness; rather woolly in his writings (partly because of his curious mannered English); a kind of highly intelligent crank. And there was also his allusiveness, not to say elusiveness - one of his women friends commented that "his mind darted here and there and everywhere like a flame always out of reach."

These were - and are - all difficulties to me in assessing him and they are shared by many of his later students and readers. But one has to consider the probability that like his thinking diagrams his thinking did not follow a line - it was not linear, it was multi-directional. When criticised by his Fabian friends about his explanatory diagrams he retorted that the best way of expressing thought was not necessarily linear; and that they themselves were dominated by *their* long-accepted idea of a thinking-machine, *their* device for expressing complicated thought by placing words in a line left to right and line below line. Writing, in short, as in this monograph!

At the end and now I see him as a formidable and courageous thinker (and realist) - and only a crank in his inability to give up.

Not the least demonstration of his essential realism was the understanding compassion of his attitude to the "workers" gained from studying their condition and environment, clear of political party cant, e.g. his comments on the exploitation by the Clydeside shipyard platers of their fellow-workers, their labourers, at the height of Britain's Industrial Revolution. Or when at the same period he contemplated the huge destruction of physical environment; and nevertheless said: "we should not so much be concerned about the degradation of our environment as the degradation of our people . . ."

It does not require much penetration to apply this to, for example, the inadequate and positively bad housing policies which were followed after the Second World War in spite of the proposals of the Clyde Valley Plan. The degrading consequences, human and physical, can be seen very clearly, and at their worst, in the peripheral housing estates in such cities as Glasgow - now a major socio-economic problem.[1] All commentators on Geddes have pointed to his belief in "conservative surgery" in the redevelopment of the people's environment. In his own words, his plea was always "to give human beings, if forced to move, at least the same care as when one transplants flowers." And this meant, as Boardman has pointed out, that "such care also means conserving their personal, cultural and religious landmarks."

As a biologist he recognised that the wealth of a nation must not be judged solely by the narrower economic and political considerations but by the health and decency and education of its people - his "quality, not quantity" theme. We still have to learn this, but Geddes saw it and was prepared to say it and to point to

---

1) I emerged from my chairmanship of the Glasgow Housing Inquiry of 1985-86 a deeply affected and puzzled man, looking for methods of social approach not yet on the horizon, but adumbrated in the "degradation" theme of Geddes as biologist-planner, and requiring an acceptable "social engineering" that goes deep into the heart of Education. Here I am walking at the end of the road where he ended.

its consequences long ago in "his early ecological warning". In a paper given to the Royal Society of Edinburgh in 1884 he said:

"Thus, in the case, when any given environment or function, however apparently 'productive' is really fraught with disastrous influence to the organism, its modification must be attempted or, failing that, its abandonment faced."

EPILOGUE

This monograph has been written in Edinburgh. To most of us there who know about Geddes, the impressive group of buildings called Ramsay Gardens and the Outlook Tower just below the Castle are, in total, one of the most spectacular sights from Princes Street. Geddes was responsible for them. But, always to me, his name evokes my memory of the stunted ill-fed men emerging from the gloom of the Cowcaddens slums that winter night in the early 1930s - the men of the Paleaeotechnic Era, the victims of our still inadequate understanding of his triad of Place, Work, Folk.

APPENDIX 1 - QUOTATIONS

These quotations have been mainly chosen from the major biographies - and some essays and articles. They give a range of sometimes conflicting views of the main elements of the work of Geddes, and readers may make of them what they will relative to this monograph itself. The appendix includes parts of the manuscript of two unpublished poems, about Geddes (*Lament for Patrick Geddes, 1 & 2*) by Rachel Annand Taylor.[1] Two of her poems (not on Geddes) have been considered good enough to be published in C.M. Grieve's *Golden Treasury of Scottish Poetry*. The other by Muriel Stuart has no known connection with Geddes but, as it happens, appears above Mrs Taylor's name in the index of Authors. Quite simply, it seemed to me to express the essence of Geddes's effect on so many people and I have ended the quotations with it.

Geddes's Written Language

In the monograph I have called his written language 'sub-Carlylean'. Here are two quotations that bear differently on this; one by Wendy Lesser: *Patrick Geddes, The Practical Visionary* (Town Planning Review, Univ. of Liverpool, Vol. 45 No. 3, July 1974).

> "Style was important to Geddes . . . As a writer about cities, he saw himself as something of a poet-prophet . . . His fantastic metaphors, his use of heavily-weighted words and the Biblical rhythms of his language all reflect this goal . . . While people have complained that the style obscures his ideas, I insist that his language is inseparable from his beliefs, representing them more accurately than any paraphrasing. Finally, I will suggest that even the obscurity, although it has prevented many of his successors from considering his ideas seriously, is singularly appropriate to his whole concept of city planning."

---

1) (I am indebted to her niece Louise Annand Taylor who holds the manuscripts.)

The other is by C.M. Grieve, a great Scottish poet, from the Notes
(P. 356) of his *Golden Treasury of Scottish Poetry*. (1940)

> "The style of Carlyle . . . was taken bodily from the Scottish
> pulpit; he was a parish minister of genius, and his English was
> not great English but great Scots-English; the most hybrid of all
> styles, with some of the virtues of the English bible, and many
> of the vices of the Psalms of David . . . He took the most difficult
> qualities of the English Language and the worst of the Scots,
> and through them attained a sort of absurd, patchwork
> greatness . . . the struggle of a Scots peasant, born to other habits
> of speech and of thought, with the English language."

Evolution Theory

Philip Boardman. *The Worlds of Patrick Geddes*, (1978)(Pp 117-118):

> "Yet Geddes's unshakeable faith in life ran all through his
> writings before and after and in the *Evolution of Sex*. He did not
> share that unobservant optimism which finds in animal life only
> 'one hymn of love', and admitted that much of struggle, cruelty,
> and selfishness exists among creatures as well as men. But he
> saw altruism coexistent with egoism in even the lowest
> organisms, and proclaimed the importance of cooperation as a
> factor in evolution even before Kropotkin's *Mutual Aid* . . . It is
> much for our pure natural history to recognise that 'creation's
> final law' is not struggle but love.

> "A contemporary has written: 'in the 1890s, multitudes of
> young men . . . owed their souls to the teaching of Patrick
> Geddes . . . even a noble soul like Huxley could see in life
> essentially a 'gladiator's show'. Geddes, pupil of Huxley,
> challenged the verdict in his books, in his lectures, in the flood
> of vivacious speech which leaped from him like a fountain. I
> recall the thrill which went through an audience as he traced
> the basal feature of all life to be the sacrifice of the mother for
> her offspring and closed by saying, with his usual fingering of
> the abundant locks and the phrase over the shoulder: 'So life is
> not really a gladiator's show; it is rather - a vast mothers'
> meeting'!"

Helen Meller, *Patrick Geddes* (1990) referring to *The Science of Life* by H.G. & G.P.Wells & Julian Huxley (1931).

> "The age of the grand synthesis of knowledge of life built on relatively simple definitions of Darwinian evolutionary theory was virtually over . . . But Wells had made a greater impact than Geddes with his ideas . . ." (and, later, in her comments) ". . . Both were in effect amateurs."

Cartoon in the *New Yorker* (March 25, 1991). This shows two squat and hirsute cavemen with gigantic clubs, one saying to the other:

> "*I'd be the first to say 'Repeal the harsh old rule of tooth and claw' if somebody could show me that it wasn't working.*"

Regionalism, Devolution, etc.

Philip Mairet. *Pioneer of Sociology: The Life and Letters of Patrick Geddes* (1957). Mairet quotes from a diary of C.R. Ashbee one of Geddes's colleagues on the plan for the University of Jerusalem:

> "In his garden cities movement Geddes was active primarily because he was convinced of the need for decentralisation and for devolution of political control from the great metropolitan centres; he wanted more regional autonomy and economy. A reawakening of local patriotism and a revitalised local life were pre-conditions of the higher 'etho-polity' that man would have to attain in the neo-technic age of the world. He would have deplored the tendency so much in evidence since the last war for the national government virtually to take over the development of the new towns created by enterprising groups on their own initiative. His conception of social and civic renewal was based upon local initiative and co-operation.
>
> "Geddes's own Scottish patriotism was deep, but not of the kind that flattered ordinary nationalistic sentiments either in Scotland or elsewhere. Fundamentally, it was a respect and love for regional rootedness and loyalty, for the unity of the *folk* in their *place*; that was a cause he would defend anywhere at any cost."

Philip Boardman: *The Worlds of Patrick Geddes* (1980), quoting S.K. Ratcliffe (1932):

> "'For 30 years he had talked to a seemingly unheeding world of the regional survey and what it could be made to mean. He lived to hear the phrase on the lips of county councillors and borough surveyors.'"

Professor Fleure, *The Sociological Review, Vol. 1 No. 2, Dec. 1952.*

"Geddes had a very strong urge to spread his ideas, and he was one of the first to organise summer schools and vacation courses especially to give teachers the mental refreshment many of them so greatly need . . . At his summer schools teachers sat, a little dazed perhaps, listening to endless variants of the Place, Work, and Folk theme . . . but they spread what has become the almost universal idea of regional survey as a means of education and even more as a preliminary to schemes of regional betterment. Some would consider the pioneering of regional survey as Geddes's most notable contribution to practical life."

Synthesis and his 'Thinking Machines'

Thomas Huxley:

"Ultimately, nothing is irrelevant to anything else. There is a togetherness of all things in an endless hierarchy of living and interacting patterns."

Professor J. Arthur Thomson's *Appreciation* in Amelia Defries's book (1927):

"Perhaps the biggest thing that Professor Geddes has done is what few people at present understand: he has thought out a notation. Our whole system is an intricate network of inter-relations . . . following the lead of Pythagoras . . . he has elaborated a scheme of possible relations - a thinking machine, an organon . . . false simplicity, at any rate, we may be spared from by Geddes' notation."

C.R. Ashbee again:

"Geddes's great achievement in life has been the making of a bridge between Biology and Social Science, thus giving a fresh clue to reconstruction, to civics and to the town plan. His, I think is one of the synthetic minds of our time. But he is very tiresome about it, and always when you think you are just going to get something done, when the thing is within your grasp, you hear the mocking chorus of the birds. The reality escapes you. You lean back and listen to Aristophanes."

Philip Mairet, *Pioneer of Sociology* . . . (1957) On Geddes's work in the High Street of Edinburgh and the reservations he had at the end of his work there - ending in the need for a new approach to Education:

"... as befitted his biological approach to the social problem he had begun at the bases of life before working upward: you could not begin lower down than with slum reclamation. He never thought however that poverty could be cured, or that the lot of the working classes in general could be much improved, without attacking less obvious but more dangerous evils at higher levels; it required a raising of the intellectual and moral guidance of every function of society. From this time onwards Geddes constantly urged the need for the separated workers upon the estate of mankind to take account of each other's aims and synthesis to fit the reference together, inspired by a vision of the conscious collaboration of vital, constructive, and imaginative energies, for which he adopted, and tried to popularise, the biological term *synergy*. But this comprehensive aim presupposed a new education; and it was to education that his best energies were now devoted."

Wendy Lesser: *Patrick Geddes The Practical Visionary*, Town Planning Review, Univ. of Liverpool, Vol. 45 No. 3, (July 1974),

"Such a mathematical abstract approach was the opposite of the empirical method Geddes had learned when studying biology . . . such charts contained the most obscure, most far-fetched and least practical part of his work."

This reservation was echoed by Israel Zangwill and some other commentators including the poet, Rachel Annand Taylor - which she utters later in this appendix in a hitherto unpublished poem *Lament for Patrick Geddes* (1950s).

Planning - Theory and Action

Philip Mairet *op. cit.*:

"... Men who were destined later to be in positions where they could use his services were realising the need for his vision and realism. If a Geddes had not existed at the turn of the century it would have been necessary to invent him - or something very like his methods. By the end of the Victorian era, intelligent people were not only awakening to the amount of material and social chaos accumulated by an age of industrial anarchy but were perplexed by the no less disorganised efforts to remedy its evils. There was much public spirited and humanitarian agitation for social reclamation and improvement, and increasing expenditure of both private and public money and energy upon them; but the efforts were inevitably unco-ordinated or even mutually frustrating in their effects; occasionally they suppressed one evil only to produce undesirable results elsewhere."

Wendy Lesser, *op. cit.*:

"His contemporaries saw him as a highly original thinker, and perhaps his originality frightened away his successors. For whatever reason, it remains true that Geddes's ideas had little direct impact on the course that city planning took after his death."

Philip Boardman, *The Worlds of Patrick Geddes* (1980):

"In the 1880s he was still enough of a brilliantly theorising biologist to be considered by many to be the successor of Darwin and Huxley, whereas in 1919 he was frankly a city planner and an interpreter of the condition of mankind."

Helen Meller, *Patrick Geddes - An Analysis of his Theory of Civics*, Indiana University 1973:

"He thought of himself first and foremost as a pioneer British sociologist who became caught up with the town planning movement, because it seemed to offer a practical way of implementing what he considered to be the purpose of sociology: discovering new laws of social development for the future . . . As a sociologist, however, both then and now, Geddes was completely disregarded. His 'social philosophy' was a hotch-potch of ideas which he picked up and tried, though never succeeded in welding into a satisfying whole."

His ignoring of the political dimension.

"The rapid changes during the First World War encouraged him to transform his propaganda for 'CIVICS: as applied sociology' into a crusade for social reconstruction. It was a crusade which was to cut Geddes off from the town planning movement which, to succeed, had to come to terms with the political realities within which planners could operate . . . His non-political stance has given him the freedom to perceive the significance of new knowledge in its bearing on social existence, especially the knowledge emanating from the life sciences. But for all his 'practical' bent, Geddes was hopelessly out of touch with realities. His contemporaries may have erred in their neglect of economic and social factors, the Treaty of Versailles at the end of the First World War providing a classic example. However, he in his turn over-reacted by ignoring political factors completely."

Meller ended her essay thus:

"His genius, for all his personal wishes, was not suited to the leadership of a mass movement. It lay instead in stimulating ideas in others by questioning preconceived assumptions. It was a valuable gift to the nascent British town planning movement, only counter-productive if Geddes himself was taken too seriously."

As a humorous personal reflection on Helen Meller's last sentence, my recollection of a discussion in Holland 30 years ago at a gathering of members of the International Society of City and Regional Planners: our visit was to the newly-reclaimed part of the Jjselmeer (the old Zujder Zee) on which the new town of Lelystad was being built. A British member must have mentioned Geddes and a Dutch planner of Lelystad said, with a twinkle in his eye, "Ah, yes, Saint-Patrick-Guide-Us!"

Anthony Sutcliffe, *British Town Planning: The Formative Years* (1980) on the growth of Planning Theory:

"This left the task entirely up to Patrick Geddes, who took it up with gusto and made a complete hash of it . . ."

Another angle on Action Planning -

Boardman on what Geddes meant by 'Wardom & Peacedom' and what 'Peacedom' should be about.

"Yet, instead of merely talking about 'the brotherhood of man and the blessings of peace', he demonstrated in both rural Cyprus and metropolitan Paris, that men can only be brothers and keep the peace if they have work to engage their energies, food to nourish their families and visions of a better future to challenge their minds. An adventurous, constructive peace is the only one that can compete with war and its glory: action. Therefore, said Geddes, real peace must be an unending fight against disease and slums, ignorance and economic injustice, against deforestation and waste of natural resources: such a peace means, both concretely and figuratively, that everyone must care for his garden.

To paraphrase his wise comment on Cyprus in 1897:

"Wherever at this moment two Easterners (or Africans, Americans, Asians, Europeans) are quarrelling in their poverty, or disputing resources wastefully plundered from nature, four or six or ten might soon be co-operating (reclaiming rural areas, humanising cities) in wealth and in peace."

Amelia Defries, *The Interpreter Geddes* (1927), about Geddes and a "Cinema Man" debating (as they are now called) 'the Media'! -

"Geddes: *'So I say again, you've got a tremendous instrument: why not learn to use it so that it does something?'*

'I can't take on propaganda', said the rather foggy Cinema man . . . *'But you are doing it all the time'* laughed Geddes *'. . . aren't you feeding people's minds with rubbish and unreality all the time, h'm? Isn't that doing propaganda for rubbish? And what about the propaganda for vice and crime and unreal ambitions and unnatural expenditure and silly vanities. . . ? Aren't you propagating what may cause havoc in the race all over the earth?'* . . .

Cinema Man: *'We give the people what they want.'*

Geddes: *'Have they not rather come to want what you give them?'*"

* * *

Poetry

Rachel Annand Taylor, *The Lament of Patrick Geddes – I & II*

Something of the Merlin-image, of the Mystagogue,
Of the Stargazer on the Ziggurat,
Within this last memorial monologue,
(That I, the sole chance listener, wondered at)
Mixed with that Scot, debonair and anoint
Half schoolman, half renaissance acolyte
Who, to Paris, Vienna, Mantua proved his point
On point, with wits and sword kept floriate bright.
Then like a cherubim whose wounded wings
Were failing, over the continents he broke
His vial of bitter-sweet and angry things
To cleanse the apathy of stagnant folk
Charmed and exasperated, they were both
To lapse too soon into the sin of sloth.

With rich felicity of fruits and leaves
Nurturing cities such as natural law
With springing principle of growth achieves;
Who, as with tumbrils, would proclaim a vision
Calling upon the Muses and the Gods
Brought sanctity of symbols to division
As unfastidious to his periods
He hurried; and his budding images
Pent in progression as of Chinese boxes
A dry determinism to express.
While I sighed softly: Take us the little foxes
The little rational foxes, foes of mine
That spoil the dark grape, harvest of the vine.

From another of her poems, conveying the same atmosphere as the poem below - by Muriel Stuart,

Still he saw miracles from his topless towers
And lavished pollen like his lily flowers.

Muriel Stuart, *The Seed Shop*

Here in a quiet and dusty room they lie,
Faded as crumbled stone or shifting sand
Forlorn as ashes, shrivelled, scentless, dry,
Meadows and gardens running through my hand.

In this brown husk a dale of hawthorn dreams,
A cedar in this narrow cell is thrust,
That will drink deeply of a century's streams;
These lilies shall make Summer on my dust.

Here in their safe and simple house of death,
Sealed in their shells a million roses leap;
Here I can blow a garden with my breath,
And in my hand a forest lies asleep.

APPENDIX II -
THE LETTERS OF CHARLES TAYLOR

Between the months of August 1928 and May 1929, this sole Scottish student at the Collège des Ecossais sent two letters a week to his parents. The letters, in total, give a detailed account of a 21-year-old student's reactions to Patrick Geddes, the College and its mode of operation. They have never been published and came into the hands of the Geddes Memorial Trust through Mrs Christine Hill, the daughter of Charles Taylor.

At first it was intended to publish substantial portions of the letters but eventually it was recognized that they would seriously unbalance the monograph. Their value consists in what is almost certainly the most detailed and continuous experience of a student at the College. They deal with the personality of Geddes himself and the living and working conditions in the College. They reflect Taylor's changing views on the value of the institution itself, the often unsatisfactory living conditions and the lack of system (as he saw it). Mumford and Boardman have commented in various ways on the "Student Rebellion" about conditions, and some of Taylor's letters give a more detailed view of this, almost day-to-day.

It is true to say, however, that his admiration for Geddes's fundamental qualities and genius remained a strong thread throughout. His daughter, Mrs Christine Hill, has emphasised in a letter to me that her father regarded his year there as the most important and illuminating period of his life.

Mr Allan Frazer, ex-chairman of the Geddes Memorial Trust, was kind enough to go through the letters, marking his choice of the elements of outstanding interest. I record his written comment to me at the end of the task - with which I agree: "You will get, in sequence, the growing appreciation and evaluation by the young man who turns out to be a most likeable fellow!"

The whole collection may be studied by arrangement with the Geddes Memorial Trust.

APPENDIX III - GEDDES'S *THINKING MACHINE*

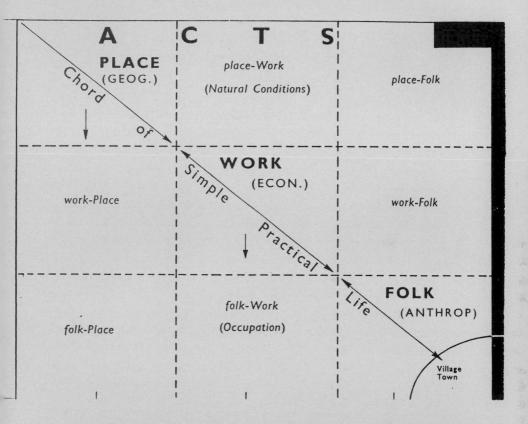

As a younger man, Geddes worked on a research project in Mexico. He became temporarily blind there. He was confined to the relative gloom indoors – but he could vaguely see the window and, dimly, its panes of glass.

He would walk to it and pass his hands over the panes. In his mind was the Place, Work, Folk triad of Le Play. He applied the words diagonally downwards to the right, and named the panes as in the triad. The other panes developed into the connections between Place, Work and Folk. Above is the first 9-square diagram that grew from that, e.g. Work Place, Folk Place, Work Folk etc. Over the years the diagram grew as his thoughts on the inter-connections grew.

The diagram shown led to much more elaborate inter-connections. Philip Mairet's biography shows on both the inside covers a 36-square diagram. Very shortly the English words became inadequate and had to give way to invented new words largely based on Greek – his famous neologisms – some of which are now used by us often without knowing they were Geddes's inventions. His new ideas and inter-connections of thought – the synthesis of environmental thought – demanded them.

The Magic Cornet

PHASE 5

6b

Level 6 – Orange

Helpful Hints for Reading at Home

The graphemes (written letters) and phonemes (units of sound) used throughout this series are aligned with Letters and Sounds. This offers a consistent approach to learning whether reading at home or in the classroom. Books levelled as 'a' are an introduction to this band. Readers can advance to 'b' where graphemes are consolidated and further graphemes are introduced.

HERE IS A LIST OF NEW GRAPHEMES FOR THIS PHASE OF LEARNING. AN EXAMPLE OF THE PRONUNCIATION CAN BE FOUND IN BRACKETS.

Phase 5			
ay (day)	ou (out)	ie (tie)	ea (eat)
oy (boy)	ir (girl)	ue (blue)	aw (saw)
wh (when)	ph (photo)	ew (new	oe (toe)
au (Paul)	a_e (make)	e_e (these)	i_e (like)
o_e (home)	u_e(rule)		

HERE ARE SOME WORDS WHICH YOUR CHILD MAY FIND TRICKY.

Phase 5 Tricky Words			
oh	their	people	Mr
Mrs	looked	called	asked
could			

HERE ARE SOME WORDS THAT MIGHT NOT YET BE FULLY DECODABLE.

Challenge Words			
know	bread	breath	magical

TOP TIPS FOR HELPING YOUR CHILD TO READ:

• Allow children time to break down unfamiliar words into units of sound and then encourage children to string these sounds together to create the word.

• Encourage your child to point out any focus phonics when they are used.

• Read through the book more than once to grow confidence.

• Ask simple questions about the text to assess understanding.

• Encourage children to use illustrations as prompts.

PHASE 5

66

This book is a 'b' level and is an orange level 6 book band.

The Magic Cornet

Written by
Shalini Vallepur

Illustrated by
Andrew Heather

Marco was feeling sad. Buttercup the cow lived on his farm and it seemed like she was sick. She looked sad and worn. Marco visited Buttercup in the barn all the time.

Marco sat in the barn with Buttercup and started singing her a song.
"I wish you felt better," Marco said.

The next morning, Marco's sister Bella saw
that Marco was sad and needed cheering up.
She had a plan.

"Marco! I need to get some corn for dinner, so you need to come with me to the market! Go and put your boots on and let's go!" said Bella.

They went to the market. There were lots of people. They were chatting, shopping and having fun in the sunshine.

There were carts that were filled with all sorts of food. There was fresh bread, jars of olives and lots of corn.

Bella went to the corner to get food for dinner. Marco stood next to a cart and waited for his big sister.

Some carts were loaded with trinkets. Marco spotted something in the cart that looked interesting.

"That's a old cornet. No one looks at it, it so you can keep it if you like," said the market seller.

12

"It's a little worn out and it's got dust on it, but I'll take it home, thanks!" said Marco.

Bella came back with a basket of food for dinner. She got jars of olives and lots of corn. "What's that, Marco?" she asked.

"This is my new cornet! I got it at the market," said Marco.
"But you cannot play the cornet," said Bella.
"Not yet!" said Marco.

Back at home, Marco washed the cornet. It no longer looked worn out. It sparkled and looked like it was brand new.

"That looks fantastic, Marco," Dad said as he put the plates out.
"Thanks Dad, I'm going to play it tonight," said Marco.

That night, there was a big storm. Marco sat in his bedroom in the dark, thinking about Buttercup.

The rain was falling hard and there was lightning. "Stay brave out there, Buttercup. I wish that I were with you," Marco said.

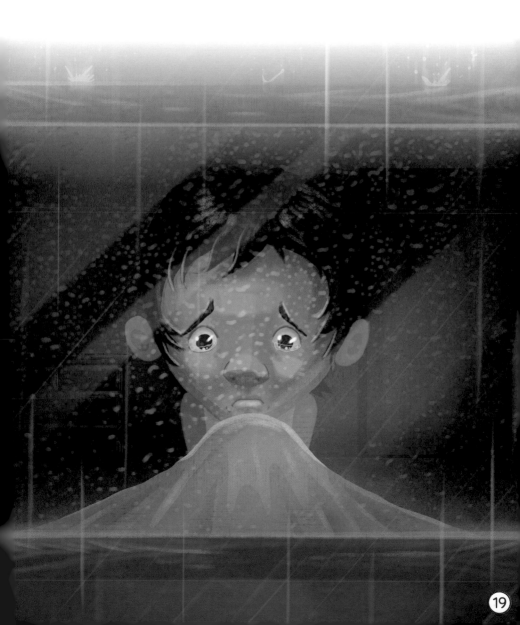

Marco picked up the cornet. He took a deep breath and blew hard!

Something magical happened! Stars and light filled Marco's dark bedroom.

"Wow! What was that? Where did those stars come from?" Marco said.

"I know! I'll go to the barn in the farmyard and show Buttercup! That will make her feel better, I just know it!" Marco said. Marco grabbed the cornet, put on his boots and ran into the storm.

Marco burst into the barn.
"Buttercup! I need you to see this. It is
magical!" he said.

Marco blew the cornet hard and the stars flew out again. Buttercup looked up at the amazing sight.

Marco stayed in the barn with Buttercup that night. The storm went away and the stars came out and lit up the night.

Marco woke up to a big shock the next morning.

A small cow had been born in the barn! Marco was so pleased that Buttercup had not been sick after all, she was just having a baby!

"This is magic," said Marco, as he stroked the small cow. "Welcome to the farm!"

The Magic Cornet

1. Why was Marco worried about Buttercup?

2. Where did Marco and Bella go?
   (a)   The beach
   (b)   The market
   (c)   The park

3. What did Marco do to the cornet when he got home?

4. How do you think Marco felt when the stars and light came out of the cornet?

5. Do you think the cornet was magic? What might you have done to help Buttercup the cow?

©2020 **BookLife Publishing Ltd.**
King's Lynn, Norfolk PE30 4LS

ISBN 978–1–83927–302–5

All rights reserved. Printed in Malaysia.
A catalogue record for this book is available from
the British Library.

The Magic Cornet
Written by Shalini Vallepur
Illustrated by Andrew Heather

An Introduction to BookLife Readers...

Our Readers have been specifically created in line with the London Institute of Education's approach to book banding and are phonetically decodable and ordered to support each phase of the Letters and Sounds document.

Each book has been created to provide the best possible reading and learning experience. Our aim is to share our love of books with children, providing both emerging readers and prolific page–turners with beautiful books that are guaranteed to provoke interest and learning, regardless of ability.

BOOK BAND GRADED using the Institute of Education's approach to levelling.

PHONETICALLY DECODABLE supporting each phase of Letters and Sounds.

EXERCISES AND QUESTIONS to offer reinforcement and to ascertain comprehension.

BEAUTIFULLY ILLUSTRATED to inspire and provoke engagement, providing a variety of styles for the reader to enjoy whilst reading through the series.

AUTHOR INSIGHT:
SHALINI VALLEPUR

Passionate about books from a very young age, Shalini Vallepur received the award of Norfolk County Scholar for her outstanding grades. Later on she read English at the University of Leicester, where she stayed to complete her Modern Literature MA. Whilst at university, Shalini volunteered as a Storyteller to help children learn to read, which gave her experience and expertise in the way children pick up and retain information. She used her knowledge and her background and implemented them in the 32 books that she has written for BookLife Publishing. Shalini's writing easily takes us to different worlds, and the serenity and quality of her words are sure to captivate any child who picks up her books.

PHASE 5

6b

This book is a 'b' level and is an orange level 6 book band.